NATIONAL GEOGRAPHIC

READING EXPEDITIONS®

IMMIGRATION

Yen's Story
From China to California

By Gare Th

Illustrated by H

D1378846

**PUBLISHED BY THE NATIONAL
GEOGRAPHIC SOCIETY**
Produced through the worldwide resources of the
National Geographic Society, John M. Fahey, Jr.,
President and Chief Executive Officer;
Gilbert M. Grosvenor, Chairman of the Board.

**PREPARED BY NATIONAL GEOGRAPHIC
SCHOOL PUBLISHING**
Sheron Long, Chief Executive Officer; Samuel
Gesumaria, President; Francis Downey, Vice
President and Publisher; Richard Easby, Editorial
Manager; Anne M. Stone, Editor; Margaret
Sidlosky, Director of Design and Illustrations;
Jim Hiscott, Design Manager; Cynthia Olson,
Ruth Ann Thompson, Art Directors; Matt
Wascavage, Director of Publishing Services;
Lisa Pergolizzi, Production Manager.

MANUFACTURING AND QUALITY CONTROL
Christopher A. Liedel, Chief Financial Officer;
Phillip L. Schlosser, Vice President; Clifton M.
Brown III, Director.

CONSULTANT
Mary Anne Wengel

BOOK DESIGN
Artful Doodlers and Insight Design Concepts Ltd.

Published by the National Geographic Society
1145 17th Street N.W.
Washington, D.C. 20036-4688

Product #4U1005083
ISBN: 978-1-4263-5076-4

Printed in Mexico

11 10 09 08 07
10 9 8 7 6 5 4 3 2 1

CONTENTS

LEAVING HOME

The United States is a nation of immigrants. These are people who have moved to a new place, leaving the country where they were born. Some people have come to escape from wars, conflict, or hunger at home. Others have come to find freedom and new opportunities. Whatever the reason, this country has grown thanks to waves of immigrants. One of these waves came from China in the 1850s and 1860s.

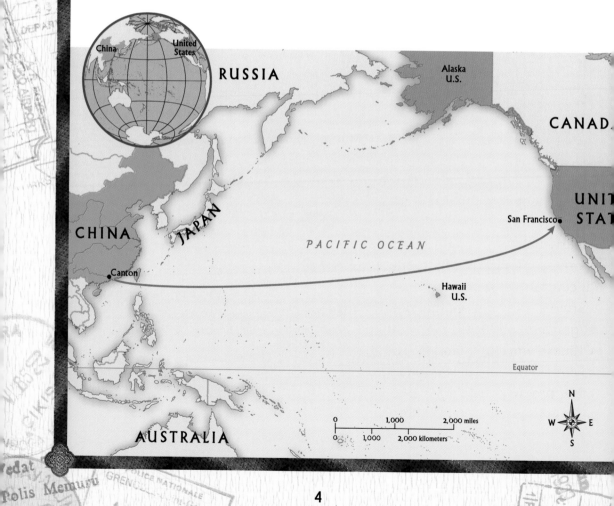

CHINA

Geography China is a country in east Asia about the size of the United States. It has many mountains, including the tallest mountain in the world, Mount Everest. In northern and western China there are deserts and high, dry plains. The hilly lowlands of southern China are warm and wet.

The People China has 1.2 billion people, more than any other country in the world. Nearly half its people are farm workers. The richest farmland is in central and southern China. Farmers grow cotton, tea, rice, sugarcane, and fruit. Many other Chinese work in factories. They make clothing, electronics, and other products. Mining is also an important industry in China.

THE LUM FAMILY

Father Lum

Five years ago, Father Lum left China to join his father in America and work on the railroad. Now the two men have a small store. They have at last saved enough money to bring the rest of the family from China.

Yen

Yen is twelve years old. He has long dreamed of the day his father would send for the rest of the family. But as the story opens, Yen is still in a farming village on the Pearl River in southern China.

6

Mother Lum

Mother is quiet but firm. She wants her children to show respect and behave properly.

Rose

Rose is Yen's younger sister. She loves poetry and painting. She wishes she could go to school with Yen. But like most Chinese girls, she must stay home and learn to sew and cook.

CHAPTER 1

The Letter

Yen stood up. His back hurt from bending over to plant the rice seeds. The seeds had to be set in the ground one by one, and Yen had been at the task for more than an hour. Even though it was spring, the sun was hot. Yen knew it would be another long day in the rice paddy. He adjusted his straw hat, hoping to keep the sun out of his face. But as usual, the hat kept slipping off his head.

Yen shaded his eyes. In the distance, he could see his uncle prodding the water buffalo along the field. Everyone here in southern China depended on rice. They ate it with every meal. Yen's family worked hard to grow the crop. Even his sister and mother helped in the fields. The work was hard, but Yen knew that his family was lucky—for they owned their own land.

Several years before, Yen's father and grandfather had left their small village in the Chinese region of Canton.

They had traveled across the ocean to "Gum Shan" or Gold Mountain. That is what the Chinese called America. Grandfather had left ten years ago, in 1859. He had gone in hope of finding gold. Five years later, Yen's father had left to help build the railroad. Now the two men ran a grocery store together.

Each day, Yen hoped for a letter telling him and his family to join the two men in America. His father had vowed to send for them. Yen knew his father would not forget a promise.

In the meantime, Father sent money back home to China. It would arrive from time to time in a letter along with news of life in America. Yen always looked forward to hearing from his father, but the money was important too. It had changed his family's life. In the first year that his father was gone, Yen's family was able to buy land. They no longer had to rent it. The second year, they built a two-room mud home of their very own. Then the next year, they bought an ox and more seeds. By the fourth year, they were growing enough precious rice to feed the family and were able to sell some too. Such a difference that money from America had made!

But now the family needed more than money. They needed to leave China. Yen hoped his father would hurry and send for them. China was no longer a safe place to live. It was 1869, and many people were unhappy with the Emperor Qing. He was a Manchu leader. Even though the Manchu had been ruling China for more than 200 years, the Chinese still had not accepted them. Many thought of them as conquerors, not Chinese, and so people resented them.

Rebels were fighting against the emperor. They called themselves the Red Turbans. They had been fighting since before Yen was born. But now the fighting seemed to be getting fiercer. The battles had spread to the countryside. People in Yen's village were scared. One town across the river had been burned. Yen and his family had seen the smoke from their home. Even worse, young boys in the area had been forced to fight for the rebels. Yen was worried that he would have to fight for them too.

There were other problems in China as well. The Pearl River Delta seemed green and beautiful, but there had been no rain for two months. Fields were drying up and turning brown. Yen's uncle had built a waterwheel. It was a clackety old machine, but it kept their small field wet enough to grow rice. Other families were not so lucky. If rain didn't come soon, the rice crops would fail. Many families would be without food. And no one would have money to buy Yen's rice either.

Yen had written his father about the rebels and the drought. His father had promised to send for them with haste. Just as soon as Yen's father and grandfather had saved enough money for the five tickets, Yen's family could leave. Yen knew it would be hard to get the whole family out of China safely, but he trusted his father to make it happen. Each day he prayed that the letter would arrive telling them to sell their farm and come to Gold Mountain.

As he stood in the field and thought of the troubles, Yen shook his head slowly. He heard his sister and mother calling him. "Just a minute," he shouted. He had one more row of seeds to plant. He quickly finished and walked through the wet field to join his family for lunch. They would eat in the field as they often did.

"It's a hot day," said Yen. He smiled at his sister as she poured water over her head to cool herself down. Her blue cloth pants and shirt dried quickly in the blazing sun.

"Rose, do behave," her mother scolded. Rose turned to her brother and rolled her eyes. She often struggled to obey her mother's rules, of which there were many. Rose longed for the same opportunities that her brother had. But she was a girl, and things were different for girls.

Over lunch, Rose chattered away like a cuckoo bird. Yen did not listen, but simply nodded his head and said, "Yes, Sister," every so often. His mother sat quietly and ate her rice and steamed fish. Her chopsticks moved quickly and gracefully.

"Yen, finish your lunch. Then you must go to school," she said. Yen nodded. He knew he was lucky that some of the money his father sent paid for his schooling, but he sometimes wondered if it was necessary. Why did he have to learn about the Emperor Qing and his ancestors? Why would he need to know poetry? Yen preferred playing games outside with his friends over sitting inside and listening to the teacher lecture.

"I wish I could go to school," sighed Rose. She said this every time that school was mentioned. Rose was smart, but very few girls in China were allowed to go to school. Only girls from wealthy families were educated, and they were often tutored at home. Rose had pestered Yen until he had taught her to read and write. She wrote poetry and drew pictures well. Maybe in America Rose could go to school.

"Rose, you have to learn to be a lady. You must learn to sew, cook, and clean," their mother lectured. "It is the only way you will find a husband."

Yen shook his head. He knew this battle between them would never end.

Mother put down her chopsticks. "Come, Rose. I have some stitching for you to do," she said.

"I hope I don't sew my fingers together," muttered Rose with a wry smile. She helped her mother gather up their dishes and lunch pails. "Learn a new poem at school for me, Yen."

"I will," he promised.

Yen trudged up the hill to the school. At the top, he paused and watched his mother and sister make their way home. Their small mud house was only a short walk from the field, but Yen wanted to make sure they arrived. Even in the countryside, people were no longer safe.

Once they entered the house, Yen raced to the schoolyard and greeted his friends. Together they walked into the one-room school. They went quickly to their desks. Before they sat, they bowed to their teacher. Yen liked their teacher. His small black eyes crinkled when he recited poetry, and his voice became deep and loud when he talked about great Chinese warriors and emperors.

Yen settled into his seat and recited the poem of the day, but his thoughts drifted far away to America. Were the streets really paved with gold? He practiced his calligraphy and copied a poem about the great thinker Confucius, but all he really wanted was to be writing to his father. Yen hoped the letter would come soon. It *had* to.

Later that afternoon, on the way home, Yen and his friends flew a kite. The wind whipped it around. Yen remembered learning that the Chinese had invented kites. He smiled. Maybe someday he would invent something. He looked at the brown fields and decided that a rain machine would be a good invention. If it did not rain soon, all the crops would die—and that was if the rebel battles didn't destroy their village first.

As Yen drew near to home, he heard the excited voices of his mother and grandmother. Rose was at the door to greet him.

"Yen, come quickly," she said. "We have received a letter from father!" Yen raced into the house. At last, it had arrived!

CHAPTER 2

Selling the Farm

Yen tore the envelope open with shaking hands. His family gathered around him. "Read the letter, Yen," Uncle Chang said. With his family by his side, Yen began to read.

Dearest Family,

I will keep this short. I have sent money to the ticket broker in Canton. You can trust this man. He will arrange safe passage for all of you on a boat to America. Be careful and do not deal with anyone else. I have written our neighbor, Mr. Ling. He wants to buy our farm. He will pay a fair price. Your journey to America will be long and hard. Grandfather and I will meet you at the dock. May the moon guide you safely and our ancestors watch over you.

Love,

Fong Lum

No sooner had Yen finished reading the letter than everyone started talking at once.

"We must cook. We must bring good food for us to eat," ordered Grandmother. She moved to get out the pots and start cooking.

"Grandmother, wait," said Yen. "We haven't even sold the farm yet."

"We must still celebrate. I will cook a special dinner for tonight. We will have *dou sha bao*. You love my sweet bean-paste dumplings. And we will make *shao mai* and *xia jiao* as well. Rose, come and help."

For once Rose did not complain about being asked to cook. She ran quickly to get the flour, rice, pork, and shrimp. Somehow, Yen knew these would be the tastiest steamed pork and shrimp dumplings the family had ever eaten.

"Yen, do you think I will be able to go to school in America?" asked Rose.

Grandmother cut in before Yen could answer. "No. You can take art courses, but you will help us work. School is for boys."

Rose looked at Yen and shrugged. She could still hope. Soon the two were laughing and dancing around the kitchen area. Grandmother swatted at them and told them to stop, but she had a smile on her face too. Things would be better in America. There would be no more drought or rebels to worry about—and soon they would be with Father and Grandfather again.

"Uncle?" asked Yen suddenly. "Perhaps we ought to go see Mr. Ling. We don't want him to change his mind about buying our land." He waited for his uncle's reply. Now that the letter had arrived, Yen was eager to leave China as soon as they could.

In Father's absence, Uncle was in charge of the family. But ever since Yen had turned twelve, his uncle had begun to treat Yen more like a man than a boy. Yen was even allowed to give his opinion in family affairs. He tried hard to earn the respect his uncle showed him.

"That is a wise idea, Yen," Uncle said after a moment. "Let us go pay him a visit." So Yen and his uncle set off for Mr. Ling's house. They walked in silence. But in the silence Yen's mind raced with many thoughts.

Yen thought of all the stories he had heard about Gold Mountain. Images began to fill his head. He pictured streets paved with gold glinting in the sun. Surely his family would be rich in the new country! That's what the stories said.

Yen tried to imagine what people would look like in America. He had never seen a white person, but he had heard many tales. Some Chinese said that white people had red hair like fire and blue eyes like the sky. Just as strange were their customs. Instead of using wooden chopsticks to eat, they had funny tools that made loud clanking noises. Even odder, they wore clothes that were thick and heavy.

Yen looked down at his own loose, light, cotton clothes. They were perfect for the hot sun. He would never wear heavy American clothes, he decided. Yet maybe his family would become so rich that they would no longer have to wear simple cotton clothes. Instead they would wear silk robes. In China, the richer you were, the more robes you had. Yen wondered if that was true in America too.

His mind drifted to where they would live. His father had never described the house, but Yen imagined that it was big. Maybe not as big as Emperor Qing's palace, but it would have a bright red tiled roof, a fountain in the courtyard, and many, many rooms. Yen would even have a room to himself. He wouldn't have to share with Uncle any longer.

The sound of a barking dog brought Yen back to China. His dreams faded, and Yen found himself staring at Mr. Ling's house. It was much larger and newer than Yen's. Yen hoped that Mr. Ling had enough money left to buy their farm.

Uncle respectfully called out Mr. Ling's name. As was the custom, they waited for Mr. Ling to invite them inside. Only then did they enter the house. Immediately the two

guests removed their shoes and followed Mr. Ling into
a large room that overlooked a courtyard.

The house seemed like a palace to Yen. He stared at
the lacquer bowls and fine bamboo furniture. Some of the
pillows were made from silk. Yen relaxed a little. If
Mr. Ling could afford all this, he would surely have the
money to buy their farm. But would he want to?

Mrs. Ling poured tea and then returned to the kitchen for some sweet honey cakes. Yen and his uncle waited for Mr. Ling to take the first sip of his tea. Once he did, the two guests sipped theirs. Yen liked the green tea, but it was so hot it burned his tongue. Not wanting to cause offense, Yen remained quiet even though his mouth hurt.

"How are your father and brother, Chang?" inquired Mr. Ling.

"They are fine," replied Yen's uncle politely. "And how is your son?"

"He is quite well, thank you," said Mr. Ling.

"I am so pleased to hear," said Uncle.

Yen was impatient, but the two men seemed in no hurry to discuss the purchase of the farm. Mr. Ling nibbled on a honey cake. Yen noticed that he did not let one crumb fall. When Mr. Ling had finished, he washed his fingers in a small dish of water placed by his side. Yen thought he looked like a scholar. Mr. Ling was short and thin. His gray **queue**, or pigtail, hung straight down his back. He wore an embroidered jacket over dark trousers. His white socks gleamed.

Mr. Ling looked at Uncle and waited for him to speak.

"We have heard from my honorable brother," said Uncle at last. "He wishes us to come to America."

----

queue – a pigtail or braid of hair

"That is good news for you. I have heard many wonderful tales of America from my own son." Mr. Ling smiled at the two visitors.

Yen tried to shift his legs without drawing any attention to himself. He wondered when his uncle would bring up the sale of the farm.

At last, after more tea and another bite of cake, Uncle continued, "We must sell our farm in order to go."

"Yes." Mr. Ling took another sip of his tea. Yen and his uncle held their breath as they waited for Mr. Ling to continue. "Perhaps I should buy your farm," he said. "We need some land to expand our rice fields."

He said it in such a quiet voice that Yen almost did not hear him.

Next, Mr. Ling pulled out a black silk bag. It was tied with a red ribbon. He pushed the bag toward Uncle. "Your brother suggested this price. I think it is fair."

"Thank you," said Uncle Chang. "I'm sure it is." He sipped his tea and finished his cake. "I will sign the papers for you and work the farm until we leave. Then it will be yours."

"That will be fine," said Mr. Ling. He stood and smiled. "May you have a safe trip." Uncle Chang and Yen followed Mr. Ling to the door. They bowed to him and left the house with the money bag. Once they were out of sight of the house Yen asked, "Is the bag filled with gold coins?"

Uncle laughed. "No, I'm sure they are silver. When we are home, we will see if they are good coins." The Chinese were superstitious about coins. They thought some coins would bring you luck. Lucky coins would help them safely on their journey.

Back at home, Uncle Chang teased open the small bag. Seven silver coins spilled out onto the table. They made a beautiful, pure sound. They were good coins. They would bring the family luck in their travels. Rose loved the flowers on the coins. She said that they looked like her paintings. Yen's mother sighed with relief. All was well.

The next morning, Uncle left early to sign the papers for Mr. Ling. There was no turning back now. Mr. Ling owned their farm. The family would have to make their way to America.

They spent the next weeks cleaning the house, packing, and saying goodbye to friends and relatives. One neighbor reminded them to be very careful in Canton. He had heard stories that young girls disappeared there. Rose laughed and said she would be fine. Uncle vowed to keep a careful eye on her.

The weeks flew by and soon it was time for the Lums to leave. Their tickets would be waiting for them in Canton.

Mr. Ling sent a cart and driver to take them to the port city. The family piled all of their belongings into the cart. They had packed few things—just their bedding, some extra clothes, their straw hats, shoes, and food. Yen took along a special green stone, called jade. His father had given it to him. Now Yen put the piece of jade on a thin leather band and wore it around his neck. That way he could touch it for good luck during the journey. He rubbed it with his thumb as they packed the cart.

"Sister, let me take your paints," Yen offered.

Rose shook her head and clutched them tight. "Thank you, Brother, but I will keep them close to me."

Yen watched his grandmother and mother make an offering to the ancestors, as was the custom.

"Now, we must go," said Uncle Chang. He helped the women into the cart.

"Do we have everything?" asked Yen.

Grandmother patted her waist and smiled at her family. "Yes, we have everything." Yen knew that she had sewn pieces of gold jewelry inside her belt to hide them. If she had to, she would sell them to buy food during the journey. Yen rubbed his jade and hoped it would not come to that. As the cart set off, the family looked at their home one last time. Their journey had begun.

CHAPTER 3

The Voyage

The road to Canton was long and bumpy. By the time the family arrived in the large port city, they were all stiff and tired. The city itself overwhelmed them. No one had ever ventured this far from home—not even to wish Father and Grandfather goodbye. Yen felt anxious. Everywhere that he turned, he saw crowds of people. And the sounds! Everyone was yelling at one another. They spoke in different dialects, using words and accents that Yen had never heard. Often he could not understand what they were saying.

The city was hot too. The heat, crowds, and noise made it hard to breathe. Already Yen missed the open fields of his village and the quiet of the countryside. For a moment, he hesitated. Maybe they had been wrong to want to leave China. But then he remembered the drought, the rebels, and how much he missed his father. It was good to be heading to America, he decided.

"Let us rest a moment," said Uncle Chang. "Your grandmother is tired." He led her over to a shady spot near a noisy teahouse.

"Don't these people ever stop talking?" asked Yen's mother. "They make my ears hurt."

"It is loud, but we will not be here long. I must only find the ticket broker's office and then we will board the ship," Uncle said. Yen hoped that this was true. His grandmother did look rather faint, and he knew that the crowds scared his mother. Only Rose seemed fascinated by the city.

"Look at the temple over there. See how it rises out of those buildings? I'd love to make a drawing," Rose said as she reached for her pad.

"This is no time for drawing," said Uncle Chang harshly. "Put your pad away."

Rose looked at her uncle. He had never spoken in such a tone to her before.

"He is nervous too, Rose," whispered Yen. Rose nodded. She tucked away her drawing pad.

Uncle Chang pulled out the address of the ticket broker. Then he took Yen aside. "I am going to the broker's office to pick up our tickets," Uncle said. "I need you to watch over the family. I won't be gone for long. You must keep an eye on Rose while I am away. Remember the stories, how girls from the villages sometimes disappear in Canton? It is not always safe in the city for young girls. Promise you will not lose sight of your sister."

"Yes, Uncle," said Yen. He stood guard over the family and hoped that his uncle would be quick. He scanned the crowd bustling around them.

"Look, that man is selling lemonade!" cried Rose. "I'm going to get some." Before Yen could stop her, she disappeared into the crowd.

"Rose!" cried Yen's mother. "Yen, you must find her!"

Yen raced after his sister, but she had vanished. He turned every way looking for Rose. He shouted her name. Where was she?

Panic clutched at Yen's throat. He did not know what to do. Should he go back to Mother and Grandmother or should he keep searching? He was afraid he might get lost too, if he went on looking.

As he turned to go back, Yen caught sight of Rose. She was talking to a man. Yen raced over to her side.

"What are you doing?" he yelled.

Rose looked at him in surprise. "Why are you so angry? I'm buying a *shi zi bing* for Grandmother. You know she loves **persimmon** cakes. It will make her feel

----

persimmon – a type of edible berry

29

better." Rose took the cake from the man and gave him a coin.

"You know it is dangerous here! You scared Mother half to death." Yen did not let on that he had also been scared. He stormed off, and then turned to make sure that Rose was following him.

"I didn't mean to," Rose said.

Yen only glared at her. He was not yet ready to forgive his sister. "This is not our village," he said fiercely. "You can't just race off like that. Is that clear?" Rose nodded her head meekly.

Once they were back, Mother grabbed Rose and hugged her. "Thank you, Yen."

Rose offered her grandmother the cake. "Eat this, Grandmother. It will make you feel better." Rose didn't want to be scolded by her grandmother too.

Yen began scanning the crowds for his uncle. It seemed like he had been gone for hours, although Yen was sure it had been only a short time. What if the broker did not give his uncle the tickets? Many Chinese villagers had been cheated by brokers who stole their money and did not issue any tickets. Or what if they were given tickets to a different **destination**, not America? Sometimes villagers were put on ships and sent somewhere else. Then they

----

destination – the endpoint of a journey

were forced to work on large farms on islands such as Hawaii. Yen took a deep breath. He would have to trust that his father had taken care of things.

"Yen," asked Rose after a time. "May I take out my pad and sketch some of the boats in the harbor? The smoke pouring out of the tall stacks look like a dragon's breath."

"Yes, as long as you don't run off again."

"I promise." Rose pulled out her pad and began to draw. Grandmother dozed and snored gently, while Yen's mother rested, sitting on their roll of bedding.

Yen relaxed. To pass the time, he studied people. Most were Chinese dressed in the blue clothes that farmers wore. Yen saw one or two men dressed in fine silk robes. They must be rich merchants, thought Yen. Then he saw the strangest sight.

It was a tall man. He stood taller than any of the Chinese in the crowd, and he had white skin. He did not have flaming red hair like the sun, but he did have yellow hair the color of gold. And he had a beard. His clothes seemed heavy and thick. To Yen, the man looked like a golden bear. He walked toward the Lums.

Yen backed up and stood in front of his family. The man looked at Yen and said something in a language that Yen did not understand. To be safe, Yen nodded. The man kept walking. Once he had passed, Yen let out his breath. So that is what white people looked like!

"Look, there is Uncle Chang," cried Rose. She quickly put away her pad and charcoal. Yen waved to his uncle and shouted his name. Uncle smiled when he saw his family. They were all still safe.

"I have the tickets. We must go to the dock. Stay together and follow me. Do not talk to anyone else and do not offer anything to anyone. The broker told me that people might try to take our tickets or our things."

The family jostled their way through the crowd. Yen's uncle stopped in front of a huge steamship. It had funny writing on the side of it. Neither Yen nor Rose could read what it said. Smoke curled out of a tall chimney.

"We must get in this line," said Uncle Chang. He motioned the family to join a line waiting to board the ship. Rose pointed to a red bird that was painted on the side. "That is a good sign," she said. Red was a lucky color for the Chinese and birds were good luck. The boat would carry the family safely across the ocean.

At last they reached the head of the line. Yen's uncle handed the tickets to the agent. The agent counted them, then looked carefully at each of the five travelers. He asked Uncle Chang where they were going. Uncle Chang took a deep breath and then spoke.

"We are going to San Francisco," he said. "My father and brother are there. They will give us jobs." He was only repeating what the broker had told him to say.

If Uncle Chang did not say they had family and jobs waiting for them in America, the agent could turn them away. Then what would they do?

After a long moment, the agent let them pass. The Lums found a place on deck and watched the crowd on the docks as the boat slowly moved out of the harbor. Someone set off firecrackers, and drums began to play. People on the dock shouted and waved. Yen waved back.

"Who are you waving at?" asked Rose.

"No one, just saying goodbye to China," said Yen in a soft voice. He wondered if he would ever see China again.

Their voyage took four weeks. Life on board the ship was hard. Yen hated the cramped quarters belowdecks where they were forced to sleep in wooden bunks. Each bunk was only seventeen inches apart. Yen kept hitting his head on the bunk above him. In bad weather, people often fell out of the bunks. Many also got seasick from the motion of the boat on the water. Yen could not wait to get to America. Each day was the same. They slept in cramped quarters, they ate, and they hoped for their first glimpse of America.

Yen and Rose escaped to the deck whenever possible. Neither could stand the crowded hull. Just the smell of so many people crammed into a small space was awful. On deck, Rose and Yen could breathe and move—even if they were confined to one tiny area. They could not go anywhere near the white people. One day they had seen the sailors beat a Chinese man who had walked into the forbidden area.

"Why is it forbidden to go where the white people are?" asked Rose. She looked longingly at the wide open space that the white people had on deck. Sailors served them food and cold drinks. There were no such luxuries in the Chinese section. It was so unfair, thought Rose. She chafed against the restriction, but she stayed put.

After four weeks, Yen and Rose saw an amazing sight. A giant fish leaped into the air and then dove into the ocean. The fish seemed as big as the boat. A man next to them explained it wasn't really a fish. It was a whale, and it meant that land was near. At last, their journey was coming to an end.

CHAPTER 4

A New Home

The deck seethed with passengers eager to leave the boat. Yen and his family struggled toward the gangplank with their belongings. Uncle Chang shouted to them to stay together. "Yen, hold Rose's hand!" he hollered above the din.

"You don't have to hold my hand," Rose protested. "I'm not going to run away."

"Ha! I'm not so sure," replied Yen. "Besides look at the crowds on the dock. It would be too easy for one of us to get lost."

Yen took her hand. With his free hand he clutched a bundle of blankets.

"What do you think father looks like?" asked Rose. She had been so young when he left that she could barely remember him. She had only a vague impression in her mind.

"I think he is tall like Uncle Chang," Yen replied. "He will be wearing the blue clothes that mother sent."

"Yen, all of us are wearing blue clothes," laughed
Rose. She was right. In front of them, the passengers
formed what looked like a long blue snake. Yen
wondered how his father would know them. He pulled
Rose aside and they waited for Uncle Chang, Mother, and
Grandmother to catch up with them. Soon they were
together again.

"Let's go," said Uncle Chang. "One of the men told me
how we can find your father and grandfather. Many
people from our region live near one another in this new
city. So all we have to do is listen to the people around us.
When we hear someone speaking the dialect of our village,
we follow the sound. That will lead us to your father."

On the dock Yen heard people talking in the same language used in their village. "Quick, follow those voices," said Yen. The family set off toward the voices. Yen cried out, "Father, can you hear us? It is Yen!"

He paused. Then he heard a shout in response. "I am here! Look ahead. I am holding a small red dragon."

Yen and his family pushed forward through the crowd. There by a small cart were two men. One was tall and thin and holding a red toy dragon. The other was gray-haired and older. Both had long pigtails and were wearing straw hats and blue cotton clothes.

"Father?" asked Yen. The man ran to Yen and held him tight.

The older man came forward and walked straight to Yen's grandmother. The two stared at one another for a moment and then bowed. Grandfather took the baskets from Grandmother and led her to the cart. Yen saw him reach for Grandmother's hand as they waited.

Mother ran to Yen's father and hugged him. Rose just stood there. She did not remember her father. Shyly she inched her way toward him. Uncle Chang pushed her from behind. "Go," he whispered.

Rose ran to her father and leaped into his arms. Father laughed and twirled her around as he had done when she was a little girl.

"My little bird, how you have grown!" he said. "This is for you." He handed Rose the red dragon. At last the Lum family was reunited.

They all piled into the open cart and rode toward Chinatown. The cart's wheels clattered noisily on the **cobblestones.** Yen looked around and tried to absorb all there was to see. The new city was just as noisy and crowded as Canton had been. Tall buildings lined the streets. Their glass windows reflected the sun.

Everywhere Yen looked, he saw white faces. Some of the men carried leather cases. No one used baskets like they did in China.

----

cobblestone – a type of stone often used for paving

Rose pointed to a group of white women walking in the street. They wore long dresses that flowed to the ground. The bottoms of their dresses were caked with dirt. "Why don't they wear pants?" asked Rose. "It would be so much cleaner and more comfortable."

"Americans do many things differently than we do," replied her father. "Look, we are getting closer to our own Chinatown. This is where Chinese immigrants have settled. You will see, it is like our own little city here. We have our own fire and police departments."

"Chinatown is good and safe. We take care of ourselves," said Grandfather. "We cannot trust all the white people. But the good news is that they like our vegetables."

"Don't they want us here?" asked Rose.

"We are hard workers, and we keep to ourselves. It is better that way," replied Grandfather in a serious tone. Yen and Rose looked at each other, confused. They hoped that they would be allowed to leave Chinatown, for both would like to explore the new city.

Yen noticed that the roads had become muddy. "Why are there no cobblestones here, Father?" he asked.

"The whites did not want to pave the roads for us," his father said simply.

Father turned the cart into Chinatown. It rolled past two large dragons that seemed to be guarding the area.

Inside this gate, the streets were filled with Chinese people. Some carried pails on poles, just like workers did back home in China. Chinese stores lined the streets. They had red lanterns or poles with bright yellow silk flags hanging by their doors. In one store window, Yen saw ducks hanging from hooks. In another, fresh fish. The smells were familiar too. Yen smiled. This place felt like home.

Father stopped the cart in front of a small wooden building. "We are here," he said as he opened the door. Yen and Rose raced inside. "Is it all ours?" inquired Rose.

"No," laughed Grandfather. "We rent an apartment on the first floor. You see, Chinese people cannot own property here—not even in Chinatown." Rose's face fell.

"Come," said Father. He walked quickly ahead and opened a door. Everyone crowded into the apartment.

"There's hardly any furniture," muttered Yen. He had expected the apartment to be furnished like Mr. Ling's house, but it wasn't. His family was not rich. They did not even own this place.

"Never mind. We will make it a beautiful home," said Yen's mother.

"Here, let me show you the rest of the place," Yen's father said as he opened another door. There were five rooms in all. Each room led into the next one. At the back of the apartment was a door that led to a small garden.

"I will have to share a room?" said Yen. He was disappointed but did not want to hurt his father's feelings, as he seemed so proud of their new home.

"It's only until your uncle gets married," replied Grandmother with a gleam in her eye. The family laughed. She had been in America only a few hours and already she was making plans to find her youngest son a wife. "Rose, come help your mother and me cook," commanded Grandmother. Yen laughed. No matter where they were, some things did not change.

Later, the Lums sat down and ate their first meal together in their new home. Yen looked around the low table and saw his family together for the first time in memory. This was good, he decided. As he fell asleep that night he wondered what his new life in America would be like.

CHAPTER 5

The Attack

The next morning, Yen awoke to sunlight streaming through the window. He opened his eyes. For a moment, he couldn't remember where he was. He thought he was still on the ship, but then he remembered he was home. His new home in Chinatown. He looked over and saw that Uncle Chang was already gone. It was time to get up.

"Yen, come and eat!" yelled Rose.

"Be right there," he grumbled, not yet fully awake. He walked slowly to the kitchen and sat down. He expected to have the same rice gruel that they had had for breakfast each day in China. But something new was on the table.

"What are those?" asked Yen, pointing to a small bowl of red fruit.

"Go ahead and try them. Or are you chicken?" Rose said with a smile on her face. "They won't bite you."
Yen picked one up and looked closely at it. He sniffed it.

It smelled sweet, but it was not like any fruit he knew from China. He popped the fruit into his mouth. It was soft and tasted sweet.

"So what are these fruits?" asked Yen as he reached for another one.

"They are called strawberries. Chinese farmers grow them, and we sell them in the store. Plus many other things. Wait till you see." Rose smiled, pleased that she knew something that her brother didn't. "Hurry up and finish. We have to help Grandfather."

"Where is Uncle Chang?" asked Yen as the two cleared the table.

"He is getting fresh fish at the docks. Everyone else is at the store. I'm sure that Mother and Grandmother are rearranging everything. Let's go rescue Father and Grandfather. I know how to get to the store. It's right up the street."

They ran up the street and Rose stopped in front of a wooden building. The building had stalls outside filled with fruits and vegetables. Yen's eyes lit up when he saw baskets of strawberries. "Don't even think about eating one," warned Rose. "I'm sure that both Grandmother and Grandfather have counted them." Yen looked at Rose.

She seemed more aggressive than she had in China. Maybe it was the air in the new city. Or maybe she was just gaining confidence.

A white silk flag floated in the breeze. Bright red Chinese letters proclaimed that this was the Lum Store. The door was open, but Yen saw that it was painted bright red. He hoped the red door would bring the store good luck.

The two went inside. Rose admired the shiny lacquer chopsticks that seemed to gleam and the lovely carved wooden bowls. "These are beautiful. Why don't we have them at home?" asked Rose. The ones at home were plain and wooden.

"Because we sell them to our customers," replied Grandfather as he came out of the back. "White people love them, and they pay a good price for them. I'm glad you are here, Yen. You can help your father deliver our vegetables. Listen to his directions. Once you are done, come immediately back to the store."

As Yen followed his father out of the store, he heard his grandmother ordering the others about. Father turned to Yen with a smile.

"Ah," he said. "Things are now normal. You did not know your grandmother when I was your age. She is the boss—but don't tell Grandfather I said so." He picked up his pole and pails filled with produce. The two set off.

As they walked, Father advised Yen. "Always remember to go to the back of house. Never go to the front door. It is disrespectful if you do," he said. Yen nodded, but did not understand. In China, people waited politely to be called into the house. They always used the front door, even if they were delivering things.

"Why must we go to the back?" asked Yen.

"That is just how it is here," Father replied. "It is the way of white people. You must learn their customs as fast as you can. Not all Americans want us here, so show no disrespect. Talk only if they speak to you first."

As Yen and his father worked, he saw other Chinese men and women walking to the houses. Some stayed inside.

Yen asked his father what they did. Did they live there? Yen's father laughed. "No, they work as servants. Some are cooks. Others clean the houses. At night they return to Chinatown."

It was time for lunch when Father and Yen finally delivered the last bit of produce. "Let's go to the store," said Father. "Uncle Chang should be back from the docks with fresh fish." They made their way quickly to Chinatown. Their wooden sandals clicked on the cobblestones as they walked. Yen noticed that some of the white people stared at them and gave them dirty looks. A couple of children pointed at Yen and yelled at him, but he ignored them. Father had explained that some Americans thought the Chinese were stealing their jobs.

When they arrived, Grandfather was pacing outside the store. He looked worried. "Chang is not back yet," he said in a tight voice. "Go to the docks and see what is keeping him—but be careful."

Yen and his father raced to the docks. When they arrived, they saw a large crowd of white workers milling in a circle. The men were shouting angry words. Yen started to move toward the crowd, but his father held him back. "Wait here. If I tell you to leave, you do so. Do *not* come to help. Go right back to the store and wait for us. Is that clear?" Yen nodded. His father moved cautiously toward the crowd.

He had gone only a short distance when one of the men turned and saw him. "Look, here's another one!" the man shouted. "He's come to rescue these coolies. Better think again!" He threw some tomatoes at Yen's father. Yen shouted, but his father told him to run to the store. "Now!" shouted Father.

Yen did not want to leave, but he had promised. As he fled, he saw the men pelt his father with vegetables. There was nothing he could do. Yen raced quickly back to the family store. It seemed like hours before his father and uncle slowly made their way to the store. The two were dripping from being struck with vegetables. Yen's mother ran to them.

"We are fine," said Father. But Yen did not think that they were. He wanted to ask why the white men had done this to them, but he did not. He did not want to seem disrespectful to his father and uncle.

"Go home and clean up," Grandfather said. "At least we are safe here in Chinatown."

Later that night after dinner, Yen crept to the edge of his room so that he could hear his parents, uncle, and grandparents talk. He heard his mother ask what was going on that the men had been attacked.

"The white people resent us," explained Grandfather. "They think the Chinese fishermen from the North are selling their fish cheaper. They want us to go home."

"Maybe we should," said Uncle Chang. "I do not want to fight every day."

"This is our home now," responded Father. "We shall go to the Six Companies. They are a group of Chinese merchants. They loaned us the money to start the store. They will help us decide what to do."

Yen hoped these merchants really could help. If the family could not go to the docks to get fresh fish, they would lose their store. And since they had sold all their land in China, they could not go back to China. They would have no money and nowhere to go.

"That is what we shall do," said Grandfather. Yen heard his grandmother say it was time to go to bed, so he scurried back to bed and pretended to be asleep.

The next day, Yen's father, uncle, and grandfather put on their finest clothes. The merchants of Six Companies were very important people. Dressing well was a sign of respect.

"Yen and Rose, you help Mother and Grandmother run the store today. We will be back in time for supper. Do not leave Chinatown," ordered Father. Yen had never heard him speak in such a firm voice. "You will be safe inside its gates."

Yen and Rose worked at the store. Yen thought that the day would never end. When customers asked where their fresh fish was, Mother simply shrugged and said, "No fish today. Try us next week."

Finally, it was time to go home. Yen locked up the store and they all walked quickly back to the apartment. Yen was glad they lived very close to the store and in Chinatown.

Yen's father, uncle, and grandfather arrived home just as Grandmother had finished cooking. Father had a smile on his face, so Yen hoped that it had been a good meeting. Before they sat down to eat, each member of the family took a small piece of food and offered it at the altar that Grandmother had set up in the kitchen. The offerings were for their ancestors. They would bring the family good luck.

"We had a good meeting," said Yen's father. "The merchants suggested that all of us who own stores and buy products at the docks go together once a day. That way we will be safe. Also, our police will escort us to and from the docks. Our troubles will soon be over. Until then, we must all stick together."

Everyone breathed a sigh of relief. But Yen wondered how long they would be safe before another angry crowd attacked them.

CHAPTER 6

The New Year

For a month, the police escorted the Chinese men to and from the docks. Nothing happened, although some white men continued to yell at the men. Whenever Yen and his father delivered the vegetables, they tried to finish early in the morning before the white workers were out and about. This cost them a few customers, however. Not everyone liked their deliveries to arrive so early.

After a month, the police stopped escorting the Chinese men to the docks. There had been no more trouble. At first Uncle Chang was very nervous when they went to the docks, but he relaxed after a week without incident. Father would still only let Yen leave Chinatown to make a delivery, and he never let him go alone. Yen felt like a small child, but he did not protest.

By now, Yen had picked up a bit of English. He heard the remarks that many of the white people made as he delivered vegetables. He did not like their comments about his pigtail or his clothes. The comments about his eyes hurt him the most. Many of the white children called him "round eyes" and pulled back their eyes as he walked by, but Yen did not fight back. He had promised his family to ignore them. Sometimes that was very hard.

One day Yen was working in the front of the store when a young lady came in to shop. Yen thought that he had seen her before, having tea with Mother and Grandmother, but he was not sure. Yen was about to help her when Grandmother stopped him. "No, Yen. Your uncle will see to the lovely customer. Chang, see what the young lady wants."

Uncle Chang jumped up to help the woman. She smiled shyly and told him what she needed. He bowed and got her things. The woman paid and left.

Rose and Yen watched with amusement. Grandmother had assumed the role of matchmaker. In China, she would have gone to see a matchmaker to arrange a marriage between Chang and a young woman. But here Grandmother had decided to take things into her own hands.

Yen chuckled. "Do you think Uncle Chang even knows?" he asked.

"I doubt it," said Rose. "But it doesn't matter. I just hope the woman is nice." Yen noticed that the young lady kept coming back and only Uncle Chang waited on her.

Months passed and things still remained quiet. But then in December, Yen noticed that Grandfather, Father, and Uncle Chang began to worry about money. Many white people had stopped shopping in Chinatown. Even worse, a number of their Chinese neighbors had moved away or returned home. Fewer customers came to the store.

"Why are people leaving, Grandfather?" asked Yen.

"They are moving away in search of jobs. At first, Chinese people worked in factories making shoes and cigars, but now the white people want those jobs. So the Chinese have to move. Some have gone north to fish. Others have gone south to farm."

"Are we going to have to move as well?" asked Rose. She did not want to. She had made friends and liked living in Chinatown. She had more freedom here than she had in China. True, she still could not go to school, but she could at least take lessons at the Chinese Center. Plus she had sold some of her drawings in the store.

"No, we will not move," said Father. "Things will improve in time. But we may have to take another loan to pay for Chang's wedding." His father laughed and Yen realized his father was making a joke. That must mean things would work out.

"We will all just work harder," said Grandmother, and then she began ordering everyone about the store.

Yen and Rose decided that they should get jobs. Yen could work after school, and Rose was no longer needed at the store. The two found jobs working in a restaurant down from the store. Yen delivered food and waited on tables, while Rose helped cook in the kitchen. Every little bit of money helped, especially with the Chinese New Year coming up.

Walking home from work one day, Rose and Yen began to discuss the New Year. "Just think, soon it will be New Year. Father says the moon will be full by the middle of the month. I hope he is right," said Yen.

"Do you think it will be like China, where we had dragon parades, feasts, and fireworks?" asked Rose.

"I hope so," said Yen. "I always liked the New Year celebrations back home."

Soon the Lums began to prepare for the New Year. Mother and Grandmother sewed red outfits for them all to wear. Father and Uncle Chang worked on the dragon that people in Chinatown were building. Rose had drawn sketches of the dragon, and Father had taken them to a meeting. He hoped that the people would pick him to lead the parade. The dragon was a fabulous creation. It would be more than twenty feet long. Many men would walk underneath it, carrying it through the streets.

Grandmother, Mother, and even Rose, worked hard cleaning the house. Everything had to be spotless before the New Year began. Yen helped his father give the door a fresh coat of red paint. His uncle and grandfather made a beautiful stone bench for the small garden in the back of the apartment.

Finally the New Year celebrations began. They would last fifteen days. The first morning, Yen and Rose ran into the kitchen.

"Happy New Year!" cheered Rose. Yen just smiled.
Beside their plates were shiny red envelopes. Rose and Yen
knew that there was money inside them. This meant that
they would have a successful year.

Rose and Yen had both made their own gifts for the
family. Rose gave everyone a small painting, while Yen had
written each a poem.

"These are beautiful," said Grandmother. She displayed them proudly in the kitchen. Then, as was the custom, the family made offerings to the ancestors. This time they gave them fresh oranges.

The New Year parade was exciting. Father got to lead the dragon parade. Mother and the others waved. The band played music. Yen and his friends set off fireworks.

Grandmother arranged a meeting between the Lums and Soon-Li, the woman whom Grandmother had chosen for Chang to marry. The meeting went well and so it was decided. The couple would be married in the spring.

That gave them time to make gifts for the bride's family, have Chang and Soon-Li's horoscopes done to make sure they would be happy together, and sew new red clothes to wear at the wedding. Yen asked his mother to make his a little large as he planned on being much taller by the spring.

The family ate Grandmother's sweet rice pudding, rice in reed leaves, and chicken dishes. Dishes of bamboo shoots decorated their table. The bamboo shoots were a sign of good luck and good fortune.

One day Rose and Yen were walking home from the restaurant and they talked about the New Year.

"It was even better than the celebrations in China," exclaimed Rose.

"That's only because you got some new paints," teased Yen.

"I like it here. Do you?" asked Rose.

Yen thought before he answered.

"Yes, but there are things about China that I miss. I miss knowing everyone like we did in our village. I miss my friends, even though I've made new ones. But most of all I miss the quiet of our farm," Yen said softly.

"Would you go back if you could?" asked Rose.

Yen thought for a moment. "Not to live," he said finally. "But I think I would like to visit China again someday—just to remind myself of what it's like. After all, it's where I'm from. But my home is in America now."

CHINA IN THE 1800s

Although Yen and his family are fictional characters, this story is based on actual events. In the 1800s, the people of China suffered war, famine, and heavy taxes. The rulers of China waged costly wars and expected the people to pay for them. Droughts and severe weather destroyed the rice crops. People had little to eat. Throughout the country, angry groups of rebels rose up to fight the taxes and get rid of the emperor. The fighting went on for years. When gold was discovered in California, many Chinese men decided to try their luck in America. Between 1852 and 1872, about 160,000 people left China for California.

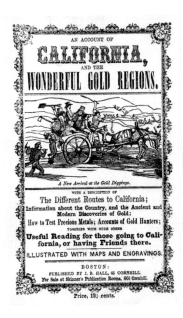

Gold Mountain—San Francisco

In 1849, gold was discovered in California. Forty thousand people arrived by ship, including men from China. Only a handful found any gold. Others built stores and businesses. The city of San Francisco grew rapidly. In the 1860s, thousands more Chinese immigrants arrived. They came to find jobs building the transcontinental railroad. By 1870, San Francisco was the tenth largest city in America.

Chinatown The Chinese who settled in San Francisco lived in a separate community called Chinatown. Even though they were in a new country, they kept traditions from their homeland. Chinatown even had its own newspapers that kept immigrants up-to-date on events back in China.

Six Companies The Six Companies was a group of Chinese merchants and storeowners. They helped new immigrants in Chinatown find jobs and housing. The Six Companies also loaned money to Chinese people who wanted  to start new businesses. Over time, Six Companies became a powerful group. It fought against laws that were unfair to Chinese immigrants.

Chinese New Year To celebrate the Chinese New Year, people decorate their houses with red and gold. Red symbolizes happiness and health. Gold stands for wealth and good luck. Children receive red envelopes with money inside. Fireworks, parades, and dragon costumes are also part of the New Year celebrations. Dragons are a sign of strength and good luck.

WRITE A PERSONAL LETTER

Imagine that you could go back in time to 1870 and visit Yen in Chinatown. What are the sights, sounds, and smells of Chinatown? Describe the place to a friend.

- Make a web like the one below.

- In each circle, write something you might see, hear, or smell in Chinatown.

- Use your completed web to write a letter describing your visit.

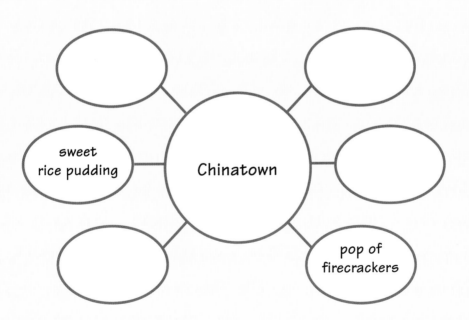

READ MORE ABOUT THE WEST

Find and read more books about the people who settled the West. As you read, think about these questions. They will help you understand more about this topic.

- What immigrant groups settled the American West?

- Who built the railroad line that brought settlers to the West?

- What caused cities in the West to grow where they did?

- How has the West changed over time?

SUGGESTED READING
Reading Expeditions
Travels Across America's Past
The West: Its History and People